SHARKS

Published by Creative Education, Inc., 123 South Broad Street, Mankato, Minnesota
56001

Printed by permission of Wildlife Education, Ltd.

ISBN 0-88682-229-7

SHARKS

Created and Written by
John Bonnett Wexo

Zoological Consultant
Charles R. Schroeder, D.V.M.
Director Emeritus
San Diego Zoo &
San Diego Wild Animal Park

Scientific Consultants
C. Scott Johnson, Ph. D.
Biophysicist
Naval Ocean Systems Center

Raymond S. Keyes
Curator of Fishes
Sea World, Inc.

John E. McCosker, Ph. D.
Director
Steinhart Aquarium

Creative Education

Art Credits

Pages Eight and Nine: Barbara Hoopes; **Page Eight: Bottom Left and Right,** Walter Stuart; **Page Nine: Top Center, Top Right, and Middle Right,** Walter Stuart; **Pages Ten and Eleven:** Barbara Hoopes; **Page Eleven: Bottom Left,** Walter Stuart; **Pages Twelve and Thirteen:** Barbara Hoopes; **Page Twelve: Top Left,** Walter Stuart; **Page Thirteen: Top Right,** Walter Stuart; **Pages Sixteen and Seventeen:** Barbara Hoopes; **Pages Eighteen and Nineteen:** Barbara Hoopes; **Page Eighteen: Bottom,** Walter Stuart; **Page Nineteen: Top Left and Bottom,** Walter Stuart; **Pages Twenty and Twenty-One:** Walter Stuart; **Page Twenty-Two:** Walter Stuart; **Page Twenty-Three:** Barbara Hoopes.

Photographic Credits

Cover: Carl Roessler *(Tom Stack & Associates);* **Pages Six and Seven:** IKAN *(Okapia);* **Page Eight: Top Right and Bottom Right,** Flip Nicklin; **Page Eleven:** David Doubilet; **Page Twelve: Top Left and Right,** Med Beauregard *(PPS);* **Bottom Right,** Ron and Valerie Taylor; **Page Thirteen:** Med Beauregard *(PPS);* **Pages Fourteen and Fifteen:** Ed Robinson *(Tom Stack & Associates);* **Page Sixteen: Top,** David Doubilet; **Middle Right,** Runk/Schoenberger *(Grant Heilman);* **Bottom Left,** Flip Nicklin; **Page Seventeen: Top Left,** Runk/Schoenberger *(Grant Heilman);* **Middle Right,** Allan Power *(Bruce Coleman, Ltd.);* **Page Eighteen: Top Right,** David Doubilet; **Middle Left,** Bob Evans *(Peter Arnold);* **Page Nineteen:** Carl Roessler *(Animals Animals);* **Page Twenty: Bottom Left,** Med Beauregard *(PPS);* **Bottom Right,** David Doubilet; **Page Twenty-One: Bottom Left,** Med Beauregard *(PPS);* **Middle Right,** Valerie Taylor *(Ardea London);* **Page Twenty-Two:** Peter Ward *(Bruce Coleman, Inc.).*

Our Thanks To: Richard Schwenkmeyer and Victoria Poma *(Mesa College);* Seaforth Restaurant; Sandra de la Garza *(Sea World, Inc.);* Dr. Richard Rosenblatt, Curator of Marine Vertebrates, and Susan Starr, Librarian *(Scripps Institute of Oceanography);* Don Pisor *(Pisor's Marine Shells);* and Lynnette Wexo.

Special Thanks to the very helpful staff — too numerous to name — in all the departments and divisions of Scripps Institute of Oceanography.

Creative Education would like to thank Wildlife Education, Ltd., for granting them the rights to print and distribute this hardbound edition.

Contents

BLUE SHARK

Sharks are a very ancient group of animals. The first sharks lived more than *400 million* years ago — 200 million years before the first dinosaurs walked the earth. In fact, the first sharks swam in the ocean before animals of *any* kind walked on land.

One of the most remarkable things about sharks is that they have changed very little in all those millions of years. The first sharks were already very good at finding food and eating it, so there has never been any need to make big changes in their design. Down through the years, sharks have remained pretty much what they always were — animals that are very capable of taking care of themselves.

Strange as it may seem, some sharks living today look a lot like the very first sharks. And even the most advanced sharks, like Great White sharks, look like sharks that lived during the time of the dinosaurs. In a way, when you look at a shark, you are looking at a living fossil.

Today, there are more than 350 different species (or kinds) of sharks. Nobody is really sure what the total number of shark species is, because the oceans of the world have not yet been fully explored. But most scientists feel that more sharks are waiting to be discovered.

Nearly all of the sharks that have been discovered so far are carnivores, or meat eaters. They usually catch their prey with their teeth. But three of the largest sharks catch their food in an entirely different way. They sift millions of small animals out of the water like big whales do. In fact, the largest of all sharks is even called the Whale shark, and it eats tiny animals that are smaller than your fingernail.

Most people fear sharks. But the more you learn about them, the more you begin to appreciate how truly wonderful they are. As you will see when you read on, sharks are full of surprises.

Sharks are different from most other fish. In fact, they are so different in so many ways that some scientists have wondered whether sharks should even be called "fish."

One of the biggest differences can be found in the skeletons of fish and sharks. Most fish have skeletons made of bones like you do. And for this reason, they are called *bony fishes*. But sharks don't have a single bone in their bodies. Instead, their skeletons are made of cartilage (CART-LIDGE), a hard and tough material that is easier to bend than bone. For this reason, sharks and their close relatives are called *cartilaginous fishes* (CART-UH-LAH-JUH-NUS).

Some of the other differences between sharks and bony fishes are shown on these pages.

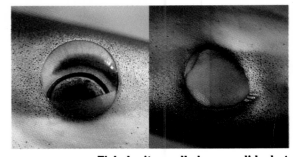

Fish don't usually have eyelids, but some sharks have *three* of them. They have an upper and a lower lid like you do, and a third eyelid that covers the entire eye and protects it.

Unlike most bony fish, sharks sink when they stop swimming. Most fish can stay up in the water without swimming because they have swim bladders. A swim bladder is like a balloon inside a fish's body. When it is filled with air or another gas, the bladder wants to float toward the surface of the water. When a fish feels itself sinking, all it has to do is add gas to the swim bladder. The force of the gas pulling up Ⓐ can be made equal to the weight of the fish pulling down Ⓑ—and the fish can maintain its position in the water.

Sharks don't have swim bladders to help them stay up in the water. To keep from sinking, they must always swim in a slightly upward direction. If they stop swimming, the weight of their bodies Ⓒ pulls them down to the bottom.

To swim, most fish have to wriggle their entire body from side to side. But a shark can get most of the power it needs from the rear fin alone. This is called the caudal (CAW-dul) fin. Some large sharks can swim very fast—up to 40 miles per hour (64 kilometers per hour).

The bodies of fish are covered with smooth scales, but sharks are covered with very rough *skin*. You can cut yourself by rubbing it. This is because the skin has lots of little *teeth* in it. The tiny teeth are called denticles (DENT-uh-culs).

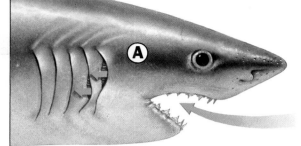

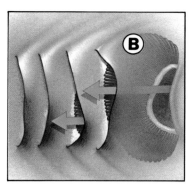

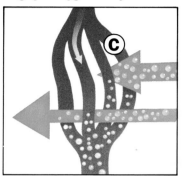

Sharks do breathe under water in the same way that fish do. They use their gills to get oxygen out of the water. To begin the process, a shark draws water into its mouth and lets the water pass over its gills Ⓐ.

Most fish have only one gill opening to let the water out, but sharks usually have five openings. Some sharks have six or seven. As the water passes over the gills Ⓑ, it comes into contact with many small blood vessels.

Most of the water in the sea has oxygen in it. As the water contacts the blood vessels, the oxygen moves from the water into the shark's blood Ⓒ. This is similar to the way that your lungs put oxygen into your blood.

Shark Denticle   **Shark Tooth**   **Human Tooth**

Shark teeth are made the same way as denticles in the shark's skin. And your teeth are made the same way. There is a pulp cavity in the middle, covered by dentine, with hard enamel on the outside.

The front fins of most fish are flexible and can be moved in many different directions. But the front fins of most sharks are stiff and can be moved in only a few directions. These fins are called pectoral (PECK-tur-ul) fins. They are stiffened with rods of cartilage and are very tough. The edges are very sharp. By changing the angle of these fins, a shark can swim up or down.

9

TIGER SHARK

Wonderful senses help sharks to find their prey. There are not many animals on earth that can locate prey and track it down as well as a shark can. Even in murky water, or in complete darkness, a shark can tell where prey is. It can tell whether the prey is hurt or not. And it can even find prey that is buried under the sand!

Sharks are not the stupid eating machines that many people think they are. They are very sensitive to everything that is going on in the water around them. And they can react very quickly to the information that their senses bring to them.

Some sharks actually use electricity to help them catch their prey. They are able to pick up very small electrical impulses through hundreds of tiny holes in their faces. The holes are called the ampullae (AM-pew-lee) of Lorenzini. All living creatures give off small electrical signals as they breathe or move, so the ampullae can guide the shark to its prey at close range.

Hearing is probably the best of all a shark's senses. Some sharks may be able to hear prey in the water from 3,000 feet away (914 meters). They use their ears to find out the direction the sound is coming from, and then turn to swim toward it.

MAKO SHARKS

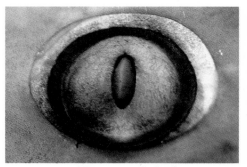

The eyes of sharks are very sensitive to light. They are made for seeing things under the water, where light can be very dim. As a shark closes in on its prey, the eyes work with all the other senses to help guide the attack.

On the sides of their bodies, sharks have lines of small holes that are sensitive to small movements in the water around them. These are called lateral (LAT-ur-ul) line organs. When fish are swimming nearby, the motion of their bodies causes small movements in the water. The lateral line organs pick these up, and the shark knows where the fish are, even if it cannot see them.

SCALLOPED HAMMERHEAD

When a shark is a few hundred yards from its prey, it probably uses its nose to find its way. Sharks have been called "swimming noses" because their sense of smell is so good. Some kinds of sharks can smell one part of blood in *100 million* parts of water. And by turning their heads from side to side, they can tell the direction that a smell is coming from.

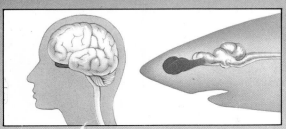

One look at a shark's brain will tell you how important smell is in finding prey. The part of the brain devoted to smell can be two-thirds of the total brain. In a human brain, the area devoted to smell is much smaller.

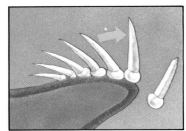

Sharks lose their teeth all the time. The teeth are not firmly set into the jaw like your teeth are. So every time a shark bites something hard, a tooth may be lost. But there are many new teeth in the jaws to take the place of lost teeth. Sometimes, it takes only 24 hours for a new tooth to grow in.

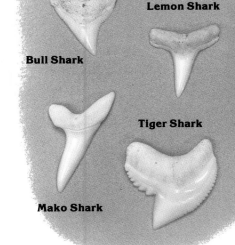

Bull Shark

Lemon Shark

Tiger Shark

Mako Shark

The jaws of a Great White shark are filled with very sharp teeth. There are 26 teeth on top that are shaped like triangles, and 24 narrow teeth on the bottom. The narrow teeth grab and hold prey, and the triangle-shaped teeth are for cutting. The edges of the teeth have serrations on them, like a saw, to help them cut more easily.

Different types of sharks have teeth of different shapes. In fact, an expert can tell what type of shark a tooth comes from by the shape of the tooth. In general, the shape of a shark's tooth has to do with the type of food it eats and the way it hunts.

①

Jaws and teeth are the things that most people think of when they think of sharks. And most sharks certainly have powerful jaws, packed with many sharp teeth. Some sharks can bite hard enough to cut through a thick piece of steel. And some sharks have hundreds of teeth that can cut like razors.

But sharks really don't use their jaws as often as most people think they do. After a big shark has had a good meal, it may go for a month or more before it eats again. Like lions and other predators, sharks usually kill only when they are hungry — and this isn't very often.

When sharks feed in groups, they sometimes seem to go crazy. Nobody is sure why they do it, but they bite everything in sight—including other sharks and even themselves. This crazy behavior is called a feeding frenzy.

Great White sharks are the largest meat-eating fish on earth today—but there were once sharks that may have been *three times bigger*. These ancient sharks had teeth that were more than 6 inches long (16 centimeters).

Scientists have named the monster shark *Carcharodon megalodon* (car-CAR-uh-don meg-AL-uh-don). It had jaws big enough to swallow a small car.

②

③

To get a really big bite of its prey, a Great White shark changes the whole shape of its head as it attacks. Normally, the mouth is located under the head ①. But when the shark starts to bite, the mouth moves to the front of the head ②. The pointed snout bends up out of the way, and the jaws rotate forward. The entire front of the head is now just a huge open mouth. As the shark bites off a chunk of meat ③, the mouth rotates back down under the body again. Sharks don't chew their food, they swallow it whole.

13

BLACK-TIPPED REEF SHARKS

The variety of sharks is really amazing. Many people think that all sharks are long and gray, like a submarine. But most sharks are nothing of the kind. There are short sharks, fat sharks, skinny sharks, and flat sharks. There are blue sharks and brown sharks, and sharks with bright spots all over them. Some have strange-looking heads and others have strange-looking tails. Some sharks have strange friends, and others behave in strange ways.

SAWFISH SKATE
Pristis pectinata

MANTA RAY
Manta birostris

ELECTRIC RAY
Torpedo torpedo

The closest relatives of sharks are the skates and rays. Like sharks, these fish have skeletons made of cartilage. Most of them live on the bottom of the ocean.

The smallest shark known to science is only 4 to 6 inches long (10 to 15 centimeters) when fully grown. You could easily pick it up in your hand.

Whale sharks are the largest of all sharks. They can be over 50 feet long (15 meters) and weigh more than 40 thousand pounds (18,144 kilograms). But these giants are usually gentle creatures. They get all of their food by sifting small animals out of the water, and rarely eat anything larger than a minnow. They have hundreds of tiny teeth in their jaws, but have never been seen biting anything.

Most sharks can only live in salt water, but there are some that can survive in both salt and fresh water. Bull sharks like this one are often found swimming up rivers, far from the sea. Nobody knows how they do it.

Even sharks have "friends." They are fish called remoras (ruh-MORE-uz) that attach themselves to a shark's skin. The remoras have special suckers on the top of their heads for holding on to the skin. They use their mouths to clean the skin, and in return are allowed to eat part of the food that the sharks catch.

Rays and skates are really just sharks that have been flattened out. The gills are on the bottom of the body instead of the sides.

Some sharks don't look like sharks. These sharks are members of the oldest families of sharks. They look like sharks that lived millions of years ago. These primitive sharks have six or seven gills on each side of their bodies.

GOBLIN SHARK
Scapanorhynchus owstoni

SAW SHARK
Pristiophorus schroederi

FRILLED SHARK
Chlamydoselachus anguineus

Some sharks live on the bottom of the sea. Like other animals that live on the bottom, they often have patterns on their skins that make it hard to see them. The Carpet shark even has a fringe on its head that looks like weeds. This shark hides on the ocean floor and waits for its prey to come along. In Australia, the Carpet shark is called the Wobbegong (WOE-be-gone).

Pilot fish also tag along with sharks. Like remoras, they eat scraps that the sharks leave. But they don't do anything for the shark to pay for their free meals.

Thresher sharks use their huge tails for herding fish together before they eat them. The tail can even be used like a bat, to stun their prey. This wonderful tail can be half the total length of a Thresher—up to 10 feet long (3 meters).

Nobody is sure why the head of a Hammerhead shark is shaped like a hammer. The eyes are placed on the end of the hammer, and this may give the sharks a better view of their prey.

Curious facts about sharks are being discovered all the time. And the more we learn about them, the more wonderful they seem. Because most people think of a shark as a mouth with a stomach attached, it's surprising to learn that the biggest organ inside a shark's body is *not* the stomach. And in spite of the great reputations that sharks have for eating, there are at least a few things that they *cannot* eat. Scientists have also found that some sharks have a strange way of saying "I love you."

Sharks really have a hard time being nice. When a male shark is courting a female, he may show his affection by biting her on the tail. Luckily, the skin of the females is very thick and it seems to heal fast.

Some sharks are hatched out of eggs. The eggs are thick and rubbery, to protect the babies inside. Many of the eggs have strings on them, like the one above. The strings get tangled with sea weed or coral and keep the egg from floating away.

Most sharks are born alive. They come out of their mothers fully formed and ready to start hunting for their food. Nurse sharks like this one usually have 20 to 30 pups that are each about one foot long (30 centimeters). Tiger sharks may have as many as 80 pups at one time. And the pups of Great White sharks may be *4½ feet long* at birth (137 centimeters).

Shark liver oil used to be the main source of vitamin A. The liver of a Basking shark can weigh over 1800 pounds (839 kilograms)— and it may contain *600 gallons* of oil (2271 liters).

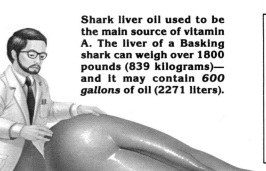

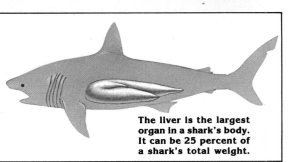

The liver is the largest organ in a shark's body. It can be 25 percent of a shark's total weight.

UGH!

There are some things that a shark cannot eat. One of them is a small fish called the Moses sole. When a shark bites a sole, the sole releases a chemical into the shark's mouth. The sharks hate this chemical so much that they immediately let go of the sole and swim away. Scientists are trying to duplicate this chemical in a laboratory, so it can be used to keep sharks away from people.

Another thing that sharks can't stomach is a pufferfish. These small fish look good to eat, and a shark may think he's found an easy meal. But once the pufferfish is inside the shark's throat, it blows up like a balloon. The pufferfish is covered with sharp spines and it sticks in the shark's throat. The shark can't pass water over its gills, and so it dies.

Amazing things have been found in the stomachs of sharks. It seems that some sharks will try to eat almost anything. Here are just a few of the things that have been found inside sharks.

People and sharks have never been friends. There are probably no other animals on earth that people fear as much as they fear sharks. Everybody has heard horror stories about shark attacks — and movies and books have made it seem like there is a big shark waiting to bite every swimmer that goes into the water.

But the facts are very different. The number of people actually attacked by sharks is very small. And most people who are attacked are not killed. It seems that sharks don't like the taste of people, and they usually go away after taking only one bite.

On the other hand, people kill over a million sharks every year. For centuries, people have used sharks for food, for fertilizer, and for other things.

Before sandpaper was invented, people used the rough skin of sharks to smooth and polish wood. Japanese warriors wrapped the skin around the handles of their swords to keep the swords from slipping out of their hands.

Indians in Florida used the sharp and hard teeth of Great White sharks as arrowheads. Natives of many islands in the Pacific Ocean used shark teeth to make harpoons and weapons.

The meat of some sharks can be very tasty, and people all over the world enjoy it. In Japan, raw shark meat is made into many interesting dishes (as shown above). And the fish in England's famous fish-and-chips is often shark meat.

NORTH AMERICA

EUROPE

ASIA

AFRICA

SOUTH AMERICA

AUSTRALIA

SOME SHARKS IN WINTER, MORE IN SUMMER

As water grows warmer, sharks migrate north

SHARKS ALL YEAR

As water grows warmer, sharks migrate south

SOME SHARKS IN WINTER, MORE IN SUMMER

Most shark attacks take place during the summer. This is because people and sharks both like warm water. When summer comes, people go swimming—and sharks migrate into the same warm waters.

The denticles can be removed from shark skin and it can be made into very strong leather. A pair of shoes made of shark leather can last four times longer than shoes made with regular leather.

Sport fishermen have found that some sharks are fine game fish. Mako sharks fight very hard when hooked and can leap as high in the air as a swordfish. The largest fish of any kind ever caught with a rod and reel was a Great White shark. It weighed 2,664 pounds (1,235 kilograms) and was almost 17 feet long (5.1 meters).

QUESTION: What is more dangerous to people—a shark or a bee?

ANSWER: A bee. More people are killed by bee stings than by sharks. Every year, hundreds of millions of people go swimming in the oceans of the world—but only about *6 people* are reported killed each year by sharks. When you consider that 50 thousand people are killed every year in autombile accidents in the United States alone, the danger of shark attack seems very small.

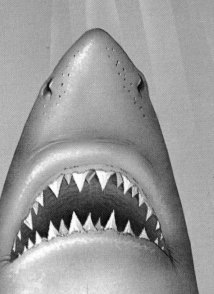

At times, some big sharks swim in very shallow water. This may be because they like warm water, and the warmest water is often found close to the beach. When people are swimming at the same beach, the chances of sharks and people meeting are increased. Sharks don't like to eat people, but they may sometimes mistake them for animals they do like to eat. A surfer in a black wetsuit, for example, looks a lot like a seal or a sea lion.

WHALE SHARK
Rhincodon typus

Sharks don't bite people very often, *but* . . .

. . . it's still a good idea to be careful about sharks when you go swimming. Here are some things you can do to help make sure that a shark will never bite you:

1. Never trust a shark. If you see a shark in the water, get out of the water. No matter how small a shark is, it may still be dangerous. Be sure to tell other swimmers that you have seen a shark, so they can get out of the water, too.

2. Don't swim in murky water. If you can't see under water, you can't be sure that there are no sharks around. Remember that sharks don't have to see you to find you.

3. Always swim with someone else. If you are alone, you will have nobody to help you if a shark attacks. It is also true that sharks are less likely to attack people in groups.

4. If you have a cut, stay out of the water until it has stopped bleeding. Blood is very attractive to sharks, and they can smell small amounts of it from very far away.

5. If sharks have been seen in a nearby area, stay out of the water. Sharks often stay in an area for several weeks — so once they have been seen, there is a very good chance that they are still swimming close by.

If you are ever attacked, there are some things you can do to protect yourself:

1. Don't panic. Sharks are excited by things that thrash around in the water. The more fuss you make, the more the shark will be interested in you.

2. Hit the shark on the nose. A hard blow on the snout will sometimes confuse a shark's senses. The shark may lose track of where you are and break off the attack.

3. Stick your fingers in the shark's eyes, or in its nostrils. This may also cause a shark to stop the attack.

4. Get to a doctor fast if you are hurt. Most people who die from a shark attack are killed by loss of blood. The sooner a doctor treats you, the better your chances of surviving are.

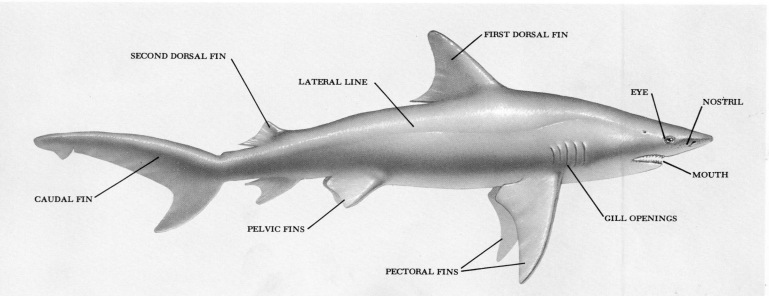

SECOND DORSAL FIN
FIRST DORSAL FIN
LATERAL LINE
EYE
NOSTRIL
MOUTH
GILL OPENINGS
CAUDAL FIN
PELVIC FINS
PECTORAL FINS

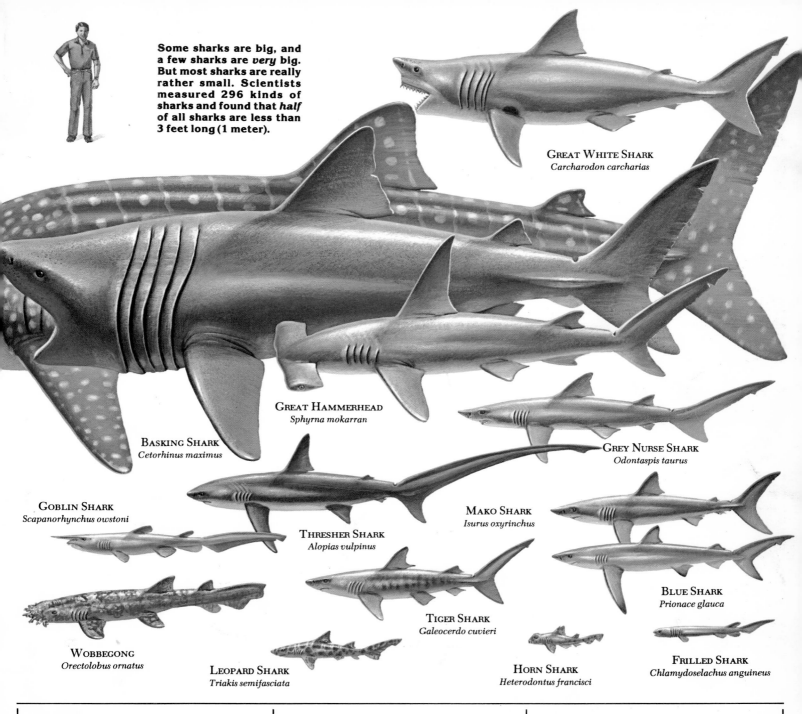

Some sharks are big, and a few sharks are *very* big. But most sharks are really rather small. Scientists measured 296 kinds of sharks and found that *half* of all sharks are less than 3 feet long (1 meter).

GREAT WHITE SHARK
Carcharodon carcharias

GREAT HAMMERHEAD
Sphyrna mokarran

BASKING SHARK
Cetorhinus maximus

GREY NURSE SHARK
Odontaspis taurus

GOBLIN SHARK
Scapanorhynchus owstoni

MAKO SHARK
Isurus oxyrinchus

THRESHER SHARK
Alopias vulpinus

BLUE SHARK
Prionace glauca

TIGER SHARK
Galeocerdo cuvieri

WOBBEGONG
Orectolobus ornatus

LEOPARD SHARK
Triakis semifasciata

HORN SHARK
Heterodontus francisci

FRILLED SHARK
Chlamydoselachus anguineus

Read about sharks

If you've enjoyed this book, perhaps you would like to read other books about sharks.

For Younger Readers

A First Look at Sharks
by Millicent E. Selsam and Joyce Hunt
Published by Walker and Company
A very simple introduction to sharks that even beginning readers can read by themselves. Teaches children about the basic parts of a shark. (Ages 4 and up)

Hungry Sharks by John F. Waters
Published by Thomas Y. Crowell Company
The ways that sharks find their food are shown in a clear fashion, with a simple text. Nice illustrations. (Ages 5 and up)

For Older Readers

Savage Survivor by Dale Copps
Published by Westwind Press
Probably the best book for older children. Packed with fascinating facts, and written in a way that's easy to understand. Scientifically accurate. (Ages 10 and up)

Sea World Book of Sharks by Eve Bunting
Published by Sea World Press
Richly illustrated with many color photographs, this book presents all the basic facts about sharks. (Ages 10 and up)

For Adults

The Book of Sharks by Richard Ellis
Published by Grosset & Dunlap
An excellent collection of shark facts, thoroughly researched and filled with the latest information.

Illustrated with many photographs and the author's own paintings. A special section at the back of the book contains biographies of some of the leading scientists that are studying sharks.

The Natural History of Sharks
by Thomas H. Lineaweaver III
and Richard H. Backus
Published by J. B. Lippincott
The best general introduction to the subject for readers who don't mind working a little. Filled with intriguing information and humor. The authors clearly love their subject, and they write about it with a lot of enthusiasm.

The Life of Sharks by Paul Budker
Published by Columbia University Press
A textbook that is nevertheless very readable. Budker knows as much about sharks as anybody, and he has filled the book with many unusual facts.

Index